This page is intentionally blank

This page is intentionally blank

Advanced Knitting

All the weaves you wish you knew.

A book by:

Bon Smith

Copyright © 2023 by Bon Smith
All rights reserved.

Please read section 1 before the rest.
You won't understand the book without it.

Section 1 - page 6
Section 2 - page 21

Section 1
Introduction:

This book is written for the optimistic, good-natured people, who find themselves in a relationship with a (usually self-titled) 'Intelligent Person' or maybe 'Alpha'. Sometimes men, sometimes women, even the non-binary. For the guys out there who have learnt so far: If someone's a dick to you, hit them. When you're living or working with someone, if you hit them, you'll always look like the bad guy. Physically violent relationships are horrible to see, the victim looks like the broken shell of a person very timid and quiet. Also, verbal abuse sucks as well.

So.. The name of the game is: M.A.D.

What does that mean?
Mutually Assured Destruction.

No one hits someone if they think they're going to hit them back. (just as hard)

Well lucky for us, from my perspective there's three kinds of abuse, Physical Abuse, Verbal Abuse (yelling, belittling, name calling), and The Unseen. What we're going to explore is unseen abuse. You could call it Psychological but I'm going to include theft, sabotage and maybe some other things as well. Things that if done well, can't usually be proven. So you can potentially get off scott-free. ;)

Ok, simply. This book is about introducing those with a god delusion to real world Karma.

Essentially
This is a book of tricks to annoy people. It has come from a lifetime of being bullied. But it came with the realisation! They don't just work on me, they work on everyone!!

I hope this makes you feel more empowered. ☺

Pre Checklist:

Ok, so the gun's in your hand..
But before you go on a shooting spree you should probably double check to see if those who've made your list actually deserve to take a shot.

What I'm trying to say is this. And believe me, this is what I've said to myself.

Ask yourself this: Are they the ones with the problem, or let's be honest, is it you/me?

Btw if your offended by anything I write and think I'm a tosser for saying it. Just a reminder, I have said all this to myself.

Ok. So how do you know?

There are many lame and boring things that people do in life, not because they are super-happy-fun-cool ideas, but because they make you a wholistically more healthy person, and what many people fail to explain for whatever reason is that 'healthy' results in 'happy'. If you're not happy you're probably not healthy and visa versa. So to keep it simple here's a checklist for you.

Checklist:

Are you exercising at least a bit each day?
(at least two 15-30 minute walks each day) the more the merrier. But the more you exercise, the more you need to eat. Otherwise you'll get super tired. If you're a super busy person two great ways to fit exercise into your day: Walking the dog or cleaning.

Do you get enough sleep?
(Roughly 9 hours a night)

Are you drinking enough water?
There's no hard and fast rule for this. But the more you exercise or the hotter it is, the more you need to drink. How do you know? Look at your wiz/piss/urine. It should be a light pale yellow. If it's clear, you've had enough, if it's obviously yellow, not enough. If it's brown, go to a doctor.

Do you eat properly?
Ultimately if it works for you, it works for you. But a tried and true method is a balanced diet. That's pretty much a bit of everything.
Soo...

An easy way to understand it is this:
Carbs are the petrol for the body.
Everything else are the tools to get the job done.

Simply:
No carbs, no energy.
None of the other things, you get sick.

Every Day should have:
Vegies (a mix of each coloured veggie is a good start)
Carbs (potatoes, rice, pasta, bread, grain, legumes)
Fruit (can't go wrong with a banana),
Dairy (cheese, milk, yoghurt, cream)
Meat (mix it up: red meat, fish, shell fish, birds, pig)
Sugary/Snacky things (quick energy) (sometimes) to get you to the next meal.
Nuts, peas, beans and mushrooms are, but definitely not perfect substitutes for meat. Diet is a science, potentially very complex, This is my simple version.

Three things essential to any diet.
Citrus fruit Lemons and Limes are the best. (high in vitamin c/citric acid, insanely good for the body)
Garlic (massively helps the body fight viruses)
Onions (helps the body to break down blood clots and other things)
Every main meal starts with onions and garlic!

Some people also find artificial additives and preservatives affect their mood negatively.

Never eat raw chicken or pork.
Chicken can often carry salmonella.
Pork often carries a tape worm that can be transferred to humans. This can cause cysts in the brain.
Don't eat carnivorous animals, they often pick up diseases from the things they eat.
(if you have to, cook it thoroughly)

If you're doing keto. Good luck, it's tough, and a little boring.

Meat (cooked), cheese, uncooked onion, uncooked garlic, uncooked leafy greens (kale/spinach) and lemon/lime juice (high citric acid compared to sugar content). The greens won't give you much energy, because the starches in them haven't been broken down (from cooking). But you will get all the vitamins and minerals your body needs.

Remember no sugary and carby things. And no fruit or milk/cream (fructose and Lactose are sugars)

Your main source of energy is protein from meat and cheese, so make sure there's enough.

Do you drink caffeine?
Coffee and Tea are a great way to get the motor warmed up in the morning and ready for the day. Also as a pick me up when you're tired.
I've tried living without caffeine. I was a moody piece of shit. I'm a better person with it.
I totally get why Muslims go on terrorist attacks, I'm like that every morning before my coffee. lol
If you're not happy, calm and energized after your tea/coffee, it wasn't tea/coffee. Forget the brand/café.

Do you read a bit?
Doesn't have to be a 1000 page novel, but a short article or two from a news paper, magazine, website, blog, Wikipedia, whatever, gets the brain turning over nicely.

Do you have a hobby?
Instead of sitting around bored, complaining that the world sucks because you're bored, do something. Anything. That's what a hobby is. Something to do when you have nothing "important" to do. Knitting, gardening, building/restoring furniture, restoring a car/bike, painting, writing, crosswords, science stuff, sculpting, gaming, fishing, whatever. Working on something that isn't bread and butter important helps me (and maybe you) to relax.
I strongly recommend getting into oil based painting. Turps works wonders to clear the air.

Have you socialised recently?

Talking shit, stupid and useless stuff. Who's dating who, who do you hate, that stupid/great tv show, your hobby. Alcohol is a pretty commonly used social lubricant. It helps relax a little and get the juices flowing. You don't need it, it just helps. It doesn't matter where you get your fix, whether it's a internet message board, a chess club, a motorcycle/car club, knitting circle, church group, band group, whatever. Chatting to other people helps to realise you are not alone! Just be wary of psychos (someone telling you to destroy people just because they/you don't see eye to eye.)

At times I've found I haven't had people to socialise with. When I need a little company, I find my favourite sitcom works wonders.

Oxygen

Ok, is there enough oxygen in your environment? This is something a lot of people don't realize is important. But high doses of oxygen can actually give you a feeling of euphoria, while low blood oxygen levels will do the opposite (make you depressed). Some cities actually have oxygen bars for this very reason!

How to fix this: get some indoor plants (indoor plants need light and water, they wont survive in a dark room) or open the doors/windows.

Drugs

Ok, drugs have been around all my life. To me it seems like they're legal. I've seen people use and stay functional and others use and fall to pieces.

A few simple rules:

Stay sober at least 80-90% of every day/week.

Choose your brands/dealer carefully.

Don't substitute drugs for a healthy lifestyle (sleep, food and exercise).

**Don't ever use Heroin, Meth/Ice or Crack.
(they make a fool of anyone who touches them)**
These drugs take over a person, they're no longer who they were, the drug controls their every action.
(It doesn't matter how smart they think they are)

Ok, but more needs to be said. Drugs are a reality of life. It doesn't seem like they're going anywhere.. Sooo, the ball's in your court. It's up to you.

Some people are good at taking drugs, some people aren't. And truth be told, alcohol falls into the same category as weed, coke and other recreational drugs. But things like caffeine or aspirin also need moderation. The question is. Does it affect you negatively? Remember what goes up must come down. The down time is when your body repairs itself.

Nowadays, a lot of drugs are prescribed by doctors. They give you advice on how to manage them. eg. How much you take and how often. For instance, speed is prescribed for ADHD.

But if you're delving into the world of recreational drugs (the ones you're not prescribed) you normally get advice from your friends or a dealer. You HAVE to be strong. In this world you have to think for yourself. Recognise the consequences and manage them.

Don't drive when you're fucked up, it's like waving a

loaded gun around after drinking half a bottle of liquor. You could also end up as a junky begging for change. Do you want that?

This is, or should be common sense. If you don't want something, say 'no thanks' politely. If they don't accept that, they're probably shitty people and a waste of your time. If you feel forced to do some, only do a small amount or pretend to do it.
Some people end up schizophrenic or with depression, others have an amazing time. If you don't want to risk it, don't do it, and maybe hang around different people.

Anyway, when you take drugs, sometimes you're in a shitty mood, realize it and manage it. Don't reply to someone's bad advice or their bad mood when you're in a shitty mood, because you'll probably regret what you say or do. Separate yourself from them. If you're always in a shitty mood when you're around them, there probably isn't much point in having that relationship (from anyone's point of view).

Managing drugs so they don't affect you negatively is an artform. If you don't think you're doing it, perhaps your choice of drugs should hit the curb. If you need help kicking it, help is out there. Google it or ask friends/family.

If you're trying to kick any major habit, go to a doctor. You'll probably need a round of antibiotics to fix things you've been ignoring.

Remember:
Suicide is a permanent solution to a temporary problem.

At the end of the day, when it comes to drugs, every now and again, take a look in the mirror. If you can't live with what you see, it's time to make a change.

Once again: Don't do heroin, meth/ice or crack. They make a fool of anyone who touches them.

Clothing:
Is your clothing appropriate for the weather? Depression and aggression can be caused by being too hot or too cold. If your clothes aren't clean they can also make you sick.

Masturbating:
No one tackles this topic better then Seinfeld. You don't need to do it from dawn till dusk, but knocking it out every day or two works for most (my opinion and others). Seinfeld really describes it well. You do it, you're more relaxed, you don't it, and you become a moody POS to be around. You can also think of your mummy and daddy bits as like a motorcycle or lawnmower. If you leave it in the back of a garage gathering dust for months or even years, don't be surprised if it doesn't work any more.

Vitamin D:
Vitamin D is another essential vitamin/hormone if you want general happiness. Simply, not enough can cause depression and moodiness. It's easy to get, you can get it added to food or in tablets or just go out in the sun for 10 or 20 minutes, with a bit of your skin exposed.

Violence:
Don't ever hit someone lightly or hard on the head (because you're smaller then them, so therefore it wont hurt them) Even smaller hits can trigger someone and put them in a state of fight or flight. It puts people into a

state of automatic response. There's a good chance they'll hit you, or try to. This response is engrained in human nature. Just a thought.

Finally. If someone is really hard on you, ask yourself this. Are they trying to toughen you up for a very stressful situation? For instance military and high end business people often bully and pay each other out a shit ton. This is done mostly to toughen each other up. Imagine this: there's a military person being shot at. Do you want them to break down into tears there and then because someone said fag, nigger, fatty or twiggy?

Humour is the best medicine.
If you don't laugh you cry.
This comes from practice.

But if you're dishing this sort of stuff out? Does anyone really need it? Life is hard enough as is.
From my experience, happy people are productive people.

Justification

The aim of this book: To create a relationship where you can relax. (that don't mean get fat, necessarily, you can still be a fitness freak, or the Michelin man, whatever you want. The aim is to create a relationship of mutual respect. Where the other person in the relationship knows they have to treat you with respect or you'll metaphorically 'punch them back'. I just heard this quote on Why Women Kill, (a tv show) Get this:

Kid: "___ hit me"
Mum: "What am I? Your body guard?.. Hit them back."

That's what it comes down to: Sometimes, if you don't stand up for yourself, you won't get treated as an equal.

A side motivation.. Because no one wants to be labeled as a wife beater.. and no one wants to be in a relationship where the other person is afraid to talk.. that would beee.. BORING!... I wonder if there's women who secretly want the ability to have physically abusive dominance over a man. I bet there is, they've probably been in or seen a relationship with physical abuse. But, as the receiver of non-physical abuse, trust me, psychological abuse, which some of these things can definitely be called might be just as tormenting or psychologically damaging.

This is all said with the aim of helping to create a relaxing relationship of mutual respect, M.A.D. Mutually Assured Destruction. That term has been borrowed from the philosophy of the big countries with nuclear weapons. (lol, it's actually Mutually Assured Diplomacy, but I think Destruction is funnier) Just remember, reading a book doesn't make you smarter, but it might make you wiser. One day you'll be in a happy relationship, you won't be doing and you might have forgotten about all these techniques. Woo! That's the dream. But the next time you come across a manipulative psycho, you'll have a few tricks up your sleeve.

Ok, this is written by someone who has a thing that swings south of the border, whatever that makes me is up to anyone who wants to use a label. I'm sure you'll agree that this probably makes me in some way a biased opinion. But to that, 'whatever', every writer is in some way biased, I'm just glad we have a voice..

But to the point of the book! Sometimes we find ourselves in a relationship with someone who is maybe not smarter, but lets phrase it as, more experienced at manipulating people. This might be a relationship you can't escape.

I suppose I'm a person that doesn't believe in any person who has the ego to think of themselves as (a) god. If that type of personality is what all these books are talking about when they say god. I am without a doubt an atheist.

This is also created with the belief in ideas like manners, or in an abstract way, maybe, Karma? I doubt I'm what you call religious in anyone's eyes, but I find some concepts pretty interesting. Karma is one of them. To me karma is.. or to me means, **you get what you deserve**.

These techniques, don't do them, unless someone is doing something to you, and they're probably best left out of the workplace (if you want to keep your job), unless you are, like, a total legend at managing people. These are more like ideas for self-defense as opposed to techniques for conquering the world.

Well.. sometimes, we don't get a choice about who we are living with and surrounded by, maybe its a super possessive partner; the social circles you exist within, maybe it's your family. When you can't remove yourself from the situation, your only option is to 'make the best of a bad bunch'.

If you're reading this guide you've no doubt got to the point where sometimes you wish you could hit someone, (who really knows how to yank your crank: eg. a family member, someone at school, someone at work, whoever). There's also a good chance you've possibly experienced some of these techniques yourself. The thing you may not realize is this: these techniques work on almost anyone, you know why? Because you can't change human nature.

Ok, so I don't want to call it this and I don't fully believe what you'll be doing is this, but for the sake of easy understanding, what you're doing is training someone; kind of in a similar way you would a dog. But not really. A better way of understanding it might be this. Imagine you're teaching someone with really underdeveloped social skills, maybe a 5 year old (or maybe someone with delusions of grandúre) how to play nice. You're teaching someone how to get along with others.

You know how people sometimes say "you should stand up for yourself", and then your thinking like. 'Yeah but you don't know this ___, a total 'see you next Tuesday', and way too smart for me. They are in a total different league to me, <u>NOT</u> worth the effort. I'll just leave them to their bullshit.' Well.. Here are some tricks for your hat... fuck that dickhead!

Once they settle down and get over the bullshit, you can start having a real relationship.

Ok, So I have a dick. But a while ago I heard a saying "The way to a man's heart is through his stomach". This came from a time when women were housewives and men made money. This isn't the case any more. In a lot of houses people with dicks are the main cook, parent or housekeepers. Well, if you're living with someone who doesn't know the first thing about diet or cooking, you're going to have a big responsibility to keep them in a good mood through giving them a healthy diet. If they're in a shitty mood, it might just be because they're eating a shitty diet. That might make their mood your fault. Just a thought.

Often (but not always) the difference between 'men' and 'women', is the way they're raised. Typically, men are raised to be gung-ho and intuitive, women are taught to follow rules and manipulate a situation. (But we all know the reverse is equally common). Well, this is a quick how-to guide to get people schooled in a little bit of self-defense if they find themselves in a highly manipulative relationship.

But.. **Choose your battles wisely!** Some people are too stupid for a truce. "you can't teach an old dog new tricks"

They'll cut off their nose to spite their face.

Don't waste your time, Get Out If You Can!

Anyway.. Enough of this badly structured rambling. Onto the book!!

Section 2

Contents:

Section:	Page
1: How to use this book	22
2: Types of People, Types of Abuse	24
3: Techniques List	25
4: The Actual Techniques	27
5: Conclusion	73
6: Notepad Section (create your own)	74

How to use this book

Ok, so you don't have to use all the ideas/techniques that are in here, but here are a few ideas to get you started. Each technique will have a name, what you're essentially doing, how to do it, and how to get over it if it happens to you; if it's possible.

Just remember, if you do it to someone and there's no real justification for doing it. See You Next Tuesday. You'll end up a lonely old wench.

The main trick is to do it until the other person stops doing whatever it is you're so pissed off about. Like for instance they may whistle whenever you're in the room, you find it annoying, you ask them 'if they can stop', they say 'stop being such a baby'. Well then, it's time to give them a taste of their own medicine. But seriously, you don't want to loose the rights that you hold dear, like talking, chewing on your pencil, talking with your hands, listening to music out loud, smoking, having an opinion etc. So it's best not to be too much of a Nazi about this stuff, they're just techniques to stand up for yourself when someone's clearly trying to bully or dominate you.

Also: **Important**. Note. Not all of these techniques are good for all kinds of abusive people. If someone is Physically abusive, you don't want to do anything they will know was done by you. <u>Because, they'll probably hit you.</u> They probably think that they know best about everything, so it's best in this situation to do things that make them doubt their superiority/intellect. They need to start questioning their own genius, so they can fix whatever it is making them such a tosser.

The trick to a working relationship is this. Talk to each other. And don't be a Nazi about someone else's opinion. If you want the freedom to think what you think and openly express it, you need to give other people that same right.

Ok, back to the book. Pick and choose, as you like. Pick something you think will work. Once they stop annoying you, stop doing it.

If they ever ask you to stop doing one of the more obvious things, deny it was intentional, and tell them 'you do it, so why can't I?'

BTW: All of these techniques are probably written down in some psychology manual somewhere. So most of what I'm saying is nothing new.

Remember: The idea of none of these tricks is to seriously injure someone. The intention is to just, take someone down a peg or two.

Important: How do you know if its working?
- You'll see it in their eyes.
- They might develop a nervous twitch.
- Their face might turn red.
- They'll say something really nasty to you.
  (laugh it off, you succeeded)
- They might accidentally hurt themselves or break something.
  (Don't annoy them when it could be serious)

Types of People, Types of Abuse

Ok, so there's more then one kind of way you can be abusive to someone, but first port of call, talk to them about it, they may not realise.

Physical Abuse: Hitting the other person when they didn't ask you to. (eg: "spank my ass", that's ok!)

Verbal Abuse: Yelling at them, calling them names. Etc.

Financial Abuse: Stopping them from getting a job. Refusing to let them control their own money. Controlling their lifestyle by threatening to take away the money they can use.

Locking them in a room or house: I don't know what this is called.

Psychological Abuse: This is briefly explored in this book.

There's probably more, time to get an education.

List of Techniques:

No.	
1:	**The Keys**
2:	**Virtual Insanity**
3:	**The Librarian**
4:	**Turrets**
5:	**A Clockwork Orange**
6:	**The Innocent Creep**
7:	**The Fucking Water Heater**
8:	**Brain Dead**
9:	**It Takes Two To Tango**
10:	**Squat Living**
11:	**Destroy The Evidence**
12:	**The Last Can**
13:	**What a bomb (Cheap Crap)**
14:	**No Sex In Weeks**
15:	**Pink Stick-Ons**
16:	**Professor Prat**
17:	**The Neat Freak**
18:	**Bums Know Best**
19:	**Here's Johnny**
20:	**Casper**
21:	**The Queen**
22:	**The Shit Stand Up**
23:	**2 bit hero**
24:	**The Old Wench**
25:	**The Kid Doctor**
26:	**Dumberer**
27:	**The Angry Housewife**
28:	**The Sweating Mechanic**
29:	**Meetings are for losers**
30:	**Rat Attack**

31:	**Doby The Midnight Taylor**	
32:	**The Mystery Shopper**	
33:	**Use The Dictionary**	
34:	**Wet Dreams**	
35:	**What's up Doc?**	
The Trip		
36:	**Brown Buscuit**	
37:	**Creeptini**	
38:	**Poker Party**	
39:	**The Vampire/Pretty Much Rape**	
__:	The List Goes On	to infinity and beyond
→	Create your own	

1: The Keys

The essence of it:
Hide things/move them into a different place

How to do it:
Ok, this one's pretty simple. Hide something they need and use regularly.
Deny Everything, they'll never be able to prove you did it (if they don't see you). Do it when they need it, (like before work)
eg:
- Turn their phone on silent and put it somewhere else.
- Keysssss! This ones a good one. Hide their keys somewhere. Back of a couch, under a cussion, under the stove etc.
Other ideas: Glasses, tablet, knitting, tools.

Important: put it somewhere they have been, so they believe they could have done it.

What happens to them: They start to question their own genius and flawless method of existence. They also might start to believe in Karma.

How to get over it:
Accept you're not perfect. Do it back.

2: Virtual Insanity

The essence of it:
Dripping taps

How to do it:
Ok, dripping taps send some people seriously insane! The constant repetitive tapping of the drip. I'm pretty sure this is a recognised form of torture. Especially if they cant get away from the sound. But, this one takes a bit of skill. You're going to need to ruin the seals on a taps washer.

Option 1: Do it up super tight, then release it. That might ruin the seals.

Option 2: Pull the tap apart and then tear the seals a bit so they leak.

<u>Turn off the water</u> for the building, tap, whatever before you can do this. Otherwise water will shoot out the tap when you open it.

What happens to them: There's real potential for insanity with this one. Especially if they I can't change a taps washer.

How to get over it:
Relax, listening to music.

3: The Librarian

The essence of it:
Coughing

How to do it:
I Love This One. Short abrupt coughs, clearing the throat is a good substitute. When they ask you to stop, cough less often but say you have a tickle in your throat. For the final course, when they're not looking the occasional clicking of the tongue, this should tick them off. Do it often, especially when they're trying to concentrate. Coughing works best if it sounds pretty much real, but the person you're trying to annoy thinks it isn't, it's all in the timing.

What happens to them:
This is a little bit like the dripping taps. But, it causes aggression instead of insanity.

How to get over it:
Do it back to them. Sarcastically, if they do it again, you do it again. Turn it into a game.

4: Turrets

The essence of it:
Loud sudden noises

How to do it:
Ok, I used to be bullied in primary school by a guy with cerebral palsy. He was very intelligent, anyway, I used to get back at him by sneaking up on him and making a really loud noise. He would freeze up and fall to the ground. Hilarious.. for a 10 year old. Anyway, loud sudden noises work on most people to a lesser extent.

What happens to them:
They get shocked or aggressive. If it is done repeatedly to them they can develop a condition. They become constantly on edge. It might be related to shell shock, I'm not sure.

How to get over it:
A decent bit of time in a relaxing and safe environment. Spending time around nonjudgmental people they can chat openly with.

5: A Clockwork Orange

The essence of it:
Whistling

How to do it:
I Love This One. I've seriously sent people insane with the use of sound. Whistling really pisses off a lot of people! My sister was pretty good at this. She used to do this shrill quiet whistle when she walked behind me. But normal whistling does the job just as well. But I came to this amazing realization, the things she did that annoyed me annoyed her just as much!! Woo. Fun times.

When they're finally willing to admit you're annoying and ask you to stop, go for it. The longer they wait to ask the deeper you'll get under their skin. Next on the menu, The Librarian.

What happens to them:
Distracts them, quiet simply probably just annoys them (and maybe a lot!)

How to get over it:
You could just ask them not to do it because you find it distracting. If that doesn't work, you could whistle at the same time, or maybe use The Librarian on them. Sometimes a little tit for tat is the only way to get the job done.

6: The Innocent Creep

The essence of it:
Unwanted touching

How to do it:
I'm not talking about grabbing someone's ass, boobs, twinky or fur burger. That's dumb, and it's called sexual harassment (that's a crime). What I'm talking about is a hand on the shoulder, the forearm when you're chatting to them. This sends some people positively nuts, they can't stand it.

What happens to them:
They get all awkward, withdrawn, tongue tied or confused. But some people might think you're hitting on them. If that's not your intention, if they ask you out or try to get intimate, say "oh sorry, I didn't mean to confuse you." ("I'm not in the mood" – *if it's your partner)"*

How to get over it:
Tell yourself 'you're not insane, they're just fucking with you'

7: The Fucking Water-Heater

The essence of it:
Turning off the hot water when they have a shower

How to do it:
This takes a little planning. You could do it with a tap if there is one (there's normally a specific hot water tap somewhere for your flat or building).
Blow out the pilot light (look it up) or you might have to read the guide to the water heater.
Plan it properly, otherwise they know it's you!

Don't turn off the cold water!! They might end up with serious burns!

What happens to them:
They get pissed!! Then you get to watch them run around in their towel trying to fix it.
If they ask you to fix it, tell them you don't know how. ;)

How to get over it:
Do it back to them. Lol or..
Develop an appreciation for the invigorating nature of cold showers.

8: Brain Dead

The essence of it:
Replace their coffee or tea with decaf

How to do it:
Replace their coffee or tea with decaf. I've been without caffeine; totally sucks and you feel the difference. Where you were an energetic go-getter, you become fatigued, unmotivated and moody. You probably won't realize at first that the coffee/tea is to blame. But you will when you change brands. Coffee shops do it to customers when they don't like them/want them coming back.

What happens to them:
Fatigued, unmotivated and moody. Maybe paranoid why their coffee isn't working.

How to get over it:
Discover the brilliance of canned energy drinks.
Or keep your caffeine on you?
Do it back to them.

9: It Takes Two To Tango

The essence of it:
Annoying them when they've just woken up

How to do it:
Myself, like most people, aren't in a great mood when they wake up. I usually haven't chilled out until I've had a shower, been for a walk, eaten and had a coffee. Then, and not until then am I ready to take on the world with a smile on my face. Anyway, if you catch someone before they do these things pretty much anything will tick them off. Opinions they disagree with, whistling, ask them to do something, give them advice; the world is your oyster. You can do it in the nicest of ways and they'll still get annoyed.

What happens to them:
Frustrated and annoyed!

How to get over it:
Avoid people when you first wake up.
Walk, shower, eat, coffee.

10: Squat Living
(The Princess Delusion)

The essence of it:
Not cleaning dishes (and denying it)

How to do it:
Don't do your dishes. Use stuff that everyone uses. When they say you haven't done your dishes, say "It wasn't me". When they say "yes it was" say "How do I know it wasn't you trying to frame me?" If you're living in a sharehouse and everyone has realized you did it. It might be time to either grow up and clean your dishes, or move to a new house.

note: Some people have an aversion to cleaning up after themselves, these people are called "Princess".

What happens to them:
There is never the equipment or space to use the kitchen. So, ipso facto, pissed off.

How to get over it:
Clean your dishes.

11: Destroy The Evidence

The essence of it:
Throwing away the things they use

How to do it:
Chuck the things they use in the bin. When they aren't looking. If they accuse you of taking it say "No I didn't, are you sure you haven't putt it somewhere accidently?" Eventually ask them, "Are you sure you didn't throw it away accidently?"
(if you want them to find it)

What happens to them:
They spend a long time looking for their stuff, probably a bit paranoid. And also a little or maybe a lot pissed off.

How to get over it:
Blah Blah Blah

12: The Last Can

The essence of it:
Using up the things they use

How to do it:
Use up the last of something they use when they're not looking. Eg: cans of baked beans, coffee, tea, milk, cheese, whatever. This is totally annoying. Especially if you're in the routine of having the same meal at the same time every day and shopping accordingly.

What happens to them:
They have to leave the house, even if they don't want to.

How to get over it:
Don't be so precious, relax and take things as they come. And never get down to the last can.

13: What a Bomb (Cheap Crap)

The essence of it:
Breaking their things

How to do it:
Break their things. Try to think of ways they could have done it without knowing. Electronics are hard. You can also break things just a little bit, so next time they use it, it breaks completely and they think they did it. Don't fuck with someone's computer, tablet or phone, there's often really important things on there. (We are trying to keep this low key, just a little fun tit for tat). If it's something really important you might end up with a knife through your stomach.

What happens to them:
Paranoid!

How to get over it:
Fix it, if you can't, buy another.

14: No Sex In Weeks

The essence of it:
Ruining their food, fucking with their food/drink (without poisoning them)

How to do it:
Putting extra salt, vinegar, yoghurt or chilly in their food, especially if they like leftovers. They'll think it's gone off, or that they're bad cooks (hehe).

What happens to them:
'The genius isn't so good at everything as what they think'

How to get over it:
Don't eat leftovers; Don't leave your cooking unattended. Rinse your veggies with water before you cook with them (that's a good idea anyway, they often have pesticides from the farm still on them).

15: Pink Stick-Ons

The essence of it:
Tapping purposefully, doesn't have to be loud, (in front of them)

How to do it:
Ok, not too difficult; works better in their line of sight, doesn't have to be loud either. You can tap a pencil on a table; I once knew a drag queen who'd do it with enormous pink stick on nails. A good substitute that makes no noise is stroking or playing with something slowly and consistently. Like slowly rubbing your finger around a glass. But if they have sex on their mind, they might get turned on by it. So it's a slight gamble. ☺

Ok, a lot of returning vets suffer from shell shock, and this is kind of related to it. Repeated, unpredictable sounds that grab your attention can cause a nervous condition.

What happens to them:
A nervous condition.

How to get over it:
Listening to music on headphones.

16: Professor Prat

The essence of it:
Giving them advice/telling them what to do
Another word for it is micromanagement

How to do it:
Whenever they're doing something give them advice on how to do it better. Eg: "You know what would be great! If you did *this* instead!"

What happens to them:
They get distracted and maybe a little short tempered.

How to get over it:
Say politely, "Sorry, I prefer it this way" if they don't accept this. Tell them "Why don't you get your own" or some variation of this. Or "There's not much point in me doing it if you're going to control my every move."

If they keep on giving you advice, put on some headphones, listen to music and ignore them.

17: The Neat Freak

The essence of it:
Reorganizing their things

How to do it:
Takes a bit of effort, but is pretty fun! Organize their things differently to the way they have done it. eg: If they have two shelves of books switch the shelves of books or flip them around so they're in mirror image; You can put their keys in a slightly different place; Organise the cutlery draw in reverse order; Change the layout of their desk so it's a mirror image.

What happens to them:
If you do this subtly and repeatedly it can make them feel seriously insane. They feel a little bit crazy! "I thought I put this there"

How to get over it:
Ask the other person if they have seen what you're looking for.
Otherwise, relax don't take things to seriously.
Do it back to them (if you know who did it) ☺

18: Bums Know Best

The essence of it:
Organizing things incorrectly

How to do it:
Take something that is organised really well and mess it up. A book shelf that is really well organised could be completely unpredictable. Alphabetical turns into non-alphabetical. A fishing tackle box, mess it all up. A knitting box, mess it all up. Whatever.

What happens to them:
Frustrated because they can't find anything.

How to get over it:
Reorganize your stuff.
Get a cup of coffee, listen to some music.

Do it back to them (if you know who did it) ☺

19: Here's Johnny

The essence of it:
Scaring/shocking them

How to do it:
This is kind of similar to Pink Stick-ons, but more dramatic. Whenever they're doing something or you're chatting to them, randomly say "Boo!" Really loud, with a dramatic movement to accompany it (hands up in front of you like you're going to grab them). Just make sure you have a smile on your face, otherwise they might knock you out.

What happens to them:
They develop a nervous condition. They might burst out laughing. They might start carrying a knife. Be careful.

How to get over it:
Laugh it off. Laughing makes you feel amazing. It's a good excuse to do it as well.
Lock the door and listen to music on headphones.

20: Casper

The essence of it:
The silent treatment

How to do it:
If they try to talk to you, ignore them, pretend they aren't there.

What happens to them:
Frustrated and maybe a little offended. They also might feel a little bit crazy.

How to get over it:
Don't worry about it, don't talk to them. There's plenty of other things you could be doing. If it's something important, that's their problem.

21: The Queen

The essence of it:
Talking down to them (being condescending)

How to do it:
Be snobby. "oh, I can imagine you'd find that a problem"; "I'm surprised you didn't know that"

What happens to them:
They get offended and yes, maybe a little pissed.

How to get over it:
Say: "Well La Di Da. Aren't you sophisticated"

22: The Shit Stand Up

The essence of it:
Teasing/belittling (its like swearing, if you have a good relationship it can be charming and enjoyable that's when it's called negging, if you don't or you're in a shitty mood it's snobby)

How to do it:
Make fun of their body. "Ok fatty"; "Absolutely Big Nose"; "look at the Oompaloompa"; "I find it hard to relate to Giraffes"; "At least I'm not a bean stalk" Or clothes. "I think that tops meant for when you're pregnant"; "I saw a bum wearing that hat"; "Aren't those shoes a little bit young for you?"; "I think that top's a little bit small for someone of your.. body shape"; "That top makes you look like you need a meal"

What happens to them:
Either they say yes to a date, or they throw their drink in your face. Have fun..

How to get over it:
Relax, they're just trying to wind you up.
Create a few comebacks to keep on call.

23: 2 bit hero

The essence of it:
Racism, sexism, prejudice of any kind. They all work in any direction. ie. woman to man, man to woman, black to white, white to black, asian to black, hispanic to asian, whatever, jew to Christian, atheist to catholic, gay to straight, gay to bi, whatever.

How to do it:
Make a joke you know the other person will hate. It's hilarious, seeing someone flip out when someone doesn't do what they're told.

What happens to them:
They blow a fuse. Can't compute. Bleep bloop.

How to get over it:
Relax, it's just a joke. Tell yourself the person doesn't actually believe it. Hopefully they're smart enough to recognize the stupidity/simplicity of these kinds of opinions. They're probably just trying to twist your tit.

24: The Old Wench

The essence of it:
Making their things stink!

How to do it:
I've been in a couple of flats where someone's done this. I used to have this old wench living above my flat. They would wipe this insanely revolting smelling stuff on our balcony (saw it happen). She said she was cleaning it. LOL.
One time in another flat this housemate left a cup of vomit or something behind a couch. It looked like vomit mixed with blood and maybe a little shit. It **STANK**!! out the place, for at least a week before it was found.
Other options.. grind up some onions, mix it with water put it in one of those spray bottles, and spray it on their stuff. You could use fish, anything rotten..

What happens to them:
Maybe they vomit?

How to get over it:
Vomit. Open the windows. Burn some scented candles.

25: The Kid Doctor

The essence of it:
Undermining (correcting)

How to do it:
When someone tells you a fact or some piece of information, correct them.
eg: "Oh, you know that's actually incorrect." Then tell them what is actually true. You can actually make things up and see if they catch you out. If you continue to disagree with them they might start to get really frustrated. Finish it with "well lets agree to disagree". That might be the cherry on top.

What happens to them:
They feel like an idiot. They get really frustrated.

How to get over it:
Relax, no one knows everything. Say "Oh, that's interesting, I didn't know that" and maybe finish that topic.

26: Dumberer

The essence of it:
Denying everything (gas lighting)

How to do it:
Do something annoying always in response to something they do regularly. When they ask why you're doing it, deny you're doing it with full honesty. Tell them they're crazy for thinking so. That's just an example.

They don't actually know. Disagreeing with them, even if they're certain they know, will send them insane. Or you can just deny doing something they saw you do. Believe what you tell them, and they will feel a bit crazy.

Dictionary definition: Gaslighting
manipulate (someone) by psychological means into doubting their own sanity.

What happens to them:
It will make them feel crazy, and frustrated. Maybe even question their own genius.

How to get over it:
Relax. Don't take life so seriously.

27: The Angry Housewife

The essence of it:
Poisoning them

How to do it:
Not a chance.
(well maybe a little, more to come)

What happens to them:
Dead, crippled or nothing (if you did it badly)

How to get over it:
More to come

If you did it, time for jail or change of name or flee the country.

28: The Sweating Mechanic

The essence of it:
Putting a hole in their brake line

How to do it:
Tell it to the cops.

What happens to them:
Dead, severely crippled or nothing (if you did it badly)

How to get over it:
Hospital.
If you did it, time for jail, change of name or flee the country.

Less deadly options:
- Put 5 to 10 litres of water in the petrol tank.
  (water sinks to the bottom and the car won't start. Hehe)
- Put a couple of bananas in the exhaust or rags or wire-wool.
  (the car will run really badly!)
- Take one of your car keys and scratch something fun in the paint.
  (it can cost 20 grand to get a paint job)
- Stick a knife in the side of their tyre.
  (let the air out first, its more quiet)
- Fuck it, pour petrol over the car and throw a match or some fireworks. lol..

29: Meetings are for losers

The essence of it:
Turn off their alarms, or change the day the alarm was set for

How to do it:
Don't do this if your worried about them loosing their job. Because they might.

Turn off their alarms. Or change the day the alarm was set for. You can often access the alarms from the lock screen of a phone. But I'm sure you can work it out.

Deny it!! don't admit, they'll never know.

What happens to them:
They look like a bit of an idiot at work. Or, like they don't take their job seriously.
Warning: They could loose their job.

If leaving someone who's been beating you, this could be a nice parting gift.

How to get over it:
Take the blame and apologize.
Choose your company wisely.

30: Rat Attack

The essence of it:
Ratting them out (Squealing like a pig)

How to do it:
Forget snitches get stiches. Society falls apart and people go feral when they think they can get away with anything. To prevent society or relationships falling apart at the seams, rat on someone you think is taking things too far.

A lot of people find this scary in this modern age where everything digital around us is monitoring us and we have no idea how or why. But, the world would fall apart without rats. Imagine a city without its subway rats!

How to do it? Leave all your electronics at home or in the car and go to a psychologist, counsellor, cop, school-teacher or preacher and **RAT THEM OUT**. These people know what to do, they'll give you advice or pass it on to people who can do something about it.

No one likes it when people have no honour in their actions. You know what to do.

Never admit to it!! They'll never 100% know it was you, there'll always be some doubt. The only way they'll know it, is if you admit to it! Say it was a look alike, something similar, you were set up or it was for a different reason.

What happens to them:
They'll get in deep shit.

How to get over it:
Karma's a bitch!

31: Doby The Midnight Taylor

The essence of it:
Altering their clothes

How to do it:
So, the key to this is that they don't think someone else did it! There's many ways this can be done. If you're a wiz with a sewing machine, you can alter their clothes so they don't fit. But that's a lot of work! There's easier ways.. Eg: cutting the stitching that holds the different parts together. These are called seams. How pissed off they get = how nice a piece of clothing you do it to. But you do need to do it to something they actually wear otherwise they won't notice. You could also slip something red in their whites washing. Everything will come out pink. Coffee stains are good. OR.. get a spray bottle, fill it with a weak solution of bleach and spray it on their clothes (the colour will fade). lol

What happens to them:
Pissed off!

How to get over it:
Fix your clothes, buy new ones or Rep' your new style!

31 ¾: Doby The Digital Taylor

The essence of it:
Altering their digital stuff

How to do it:
- Modify their work when they're not looking.
  (This is a real dick move, and takes a bit of skill to get away with/they didn't know you did it)
- Delete their profile on a game.
- Play on their profile so the level they're at changes.
- Delete programs from their watch list or watch a few episodes to mess up their progress.

What happens to them:
Pissed off!! (of differing levels)
Be careful, they could loose their job or fail an assignment. Don't be too much of a bunt, it could bite you in the ass.

How to get over it:
No idea. Deep breaths, and maybe password protect your devices/files.

32: The Mystery Shopper

The essence of it:
Buying stuff with their credit card

How to do it:
Borrow their Credit Card and buy stuff online. Send the receipts to their email so you can pretend they did it and just forgot about it. It would make it more believable if you buy things they kind of want, but you know they'd regret. Then it's easier to say that they did it and they're just being paranoid.

What happens to them:
They might start to question the belief in their own inherent superiority.

How to get over it:
It's not too difficult to protect yourself from this. Protect your passwords, and check out the credit card security settings on your bank website. Do whatever you think will help you to double check any purchases. Oh yeah, don't give people your passwords/credit-cards unless you trust they'll spend your money responsibly.

33: Use The Dictionary

The essence of it:
"If you don't want to do something, do it badly"

How to do it:
work it out.
"I'm sorry, I did try." "I have no idea what happened."

What happens to them:
"What the shit? What the shit? What the fuck do you think your doing?" "Woah, not like that!"

How to get over it:
"If you want something done properly. Do it yourself."
Maybe it's time to work on your people skills/bed side manner.

34: Wet Dreams

The essence of it:
A classic high school sleepover prank

How to do it:
Stick their hand in a bowl of warm water when they're asleep. hehe

What happens to them:
They urinate themselves while they're asleep.

How to get over it:
Wash your sheets. lol

Put a barrel bolt on your bedroom door and a lock on your window.

35: What's up Doc?

The essence of it:
Get someone sick

How to do it:
Use something they drink regularly to gargle with, and spit it back in the bottle. Give it a good mix so they can't see it.

Find a flea-ridden animal and let it sleep in their bed while they're away.

Find someone with a case of bed bugs and transfer it to their bed. With a sock or something similar.

Find what you want to get them sick with and work out a way of transferring it.

As a kid we used to throw around these seed pods called 'itchy bombs'. They had these little fibers in them that if you got on your skin would stick in and get really, really itchy. It was really hard to get them out as well.

What happens to them:

Sick, in many different ways.

How to get over it:
Move house, clean your house. Spray on deodorant is good at killing bed bugs. Spray it where you find bugs. Clean your sheets.

The Trip

This section is dedicated to drugs.

I hate many aspects of some of the hardcore ones, and don't think any person with an ounce of dignity would give drugs to any adult without their consent. But drugs are a fact of life, and they need to be talked about. Junkies are everywhere and tend to solve most of their problems with the use of drugs. A relationship with a junky is a real mind-fuck.

In reality it's quite common. Mums crush up medication and put it in their kid's food, sometimes for way longer then they should (teenagers and later). People sometimes drug their partners. People have their drinks spiked at bars, I've heard of people poisoning their parents to get their inheritance (just a rumour).

People should have the right to choose whether they do or don't take drugs, all kinds.

Consent is the basic of any real relationship and a functioning society.

36: Brown Biscuit

The essence of it:
Drugging their food

How to do it:
This can only be done with edible drugs. Some drugs are broken down in the stomach, aren't absorbed by the digestive system or are absorbed by parts of your diet. Other drugs are only available to the body when they are smoked/burnt, injected or put up the nose.

Choose the drug based on the effect you want. Sleeping pills, laxative, weed, Viagra, acid, shrooms, speed, cocaine, caffeine, heroin, meth, GHB, MDMA, ketamine etc.

What happens to them:
Depression; Inability to think clearly; blacking-out, hallucinations, hyperactivity, un-inhibited.
(it depends on the drug)

How to get over it:
Take ownership of your own diet. Aka. Cook for yourself.

Choose your housemates carefully!

37: Creeptini

The essence of it:
Drugging their drink

How to do it:
Everyone's heard of a drink being ruffied at a bar. But it can be done with any drink. A cup of coffee, a cup of tea, cordial, or chilled water.

This is quite effective as it's not likely to be absorbed by food.

Choose the drug based on the effect you want. Sleeping pills, laxative, weed, Viagra, acid, shrooms, speed, cocaine, caffeine, heroin, meth, GHB, MDMA, ketamine etc.

What happens to them:
Depression; Inability to think clearly; blacking-out, hallucinations, hyperactivity, un-inhibited.
(it depends on the drug)

How to get over it:
There are several ways of getting over a spiked drink. But, you normally need to ride out the effects that are already in effect, these tricks essentially stop you getting any higher.

- **Get your stomach pumped** (vomit)
(clean your teeth after, otherwise the stomach acid eats into your teeth)

- **Eating activated charcoal** (or crushed up regular charcoal – make sure its not on fire)
This is known to absorb many chemicals when in the digestive tract. Your body treats it like dietary fibre, "In one end and out the other".

- **Sweating it out**
Get in a sauna or hot bath, it'll encourage your body to sweat out the toxins.

- **Fighting fire with fire**
Take a drug that works in the opposite way.
If you've had too much to drink, a coffee might help. And vice versa.
An upper to reverse the downer.

- **Acid and Shrooms**
It's a special case for these. **Respiridone** was created to reverse the effects of LCD and Psilocybin. 2mg for a 70kg human. You can take more then needed and it doesn't have extreme negative side-effects. It puts people back on earth. It's cheep, but you'll need to get a prescription from a psychiatrist/doctor for these.

If your only option is to ride it out. Get yourself in a calm safe space, remove dangerous objects and listen to calming music with **NO** lyrics.

Guarding your drink
Speak to any bartender, they'll tell you it has to be done. Choose your company wisely.

The Recovery Position
If someone's super high (passed out) but doesn't look like they're going to die (they just need to sleep it off), put them in the recovery position. This is basically lying someone on their side, so if they vomit, it doesn't get stuck in their throat.

Don't have them sitting upright!

Use their legs, arms and surrounding objects to stop them rolling on their back or stomach.

Monitor them to see if they're getting any worse (eg. they stop breathing, vomit or go into a seizure)

Encourage them (don't force them) to drink plenty of water.

If you're around this all the time, take a first aid course.

38: Poker Party

The essence of it:
Sticking a needle in them
(injecting drugs)

How to do it:
Drugs don't need to be injected into a vein. A spider bite is a good example. Stick it in a muscle when they're not looking and relaxed and they'll probably just think it's a mosquito bite or just randomly itchy.

Choose the drug based on the effect you want. Sleeping pills, laxative, weed, Viagra, acid, shrooms, speed, cocaine, caffeine, heroin, meth, GHB, MDMA, ketamine etc.

What happens to them:
Depression; Inability to think clearly; blacking-out, hallucinations, hyperactivity, un-inhibited.
Maybe Dead! BE CAREFUL! You don't want to kill anyone.

How to get over it:
Karma's a Bitch!!

If you don't feel comfortable riding it out.
Go to a hospital.

39: The Vampire/Pretty Much Rape

The essence of it:
Chloroform like drugs
(rag over the mouth/spy shit)

This is pretty much rape, even if there's nothing sexual about it.
So you can be real proud of yourself if you use it. It takes no skill at all.

Personally I hate this stuff. I have had it used on me many, many times. It's like you've been raped, you have no idea what has been done to your body. But, usually in my case its for my blood, I'm healthy, no tattoos and have a useful blood type.

I live in a city ("a very liveable city") that has a serious problem with black market blood transfusions. It's how stupid people stay healthy. It seems like <u>all</u> the old, sick and disabled people are running around drugging the young/healthy and getting blood transfusions off them. How do I know? I try hard to be healthy, and it happens to me all the time. When they're successful, my immune system crashes and I feel revolting (sick) for close to a week give or take. It happens at least (or at least they try) a minimum two times a week.

Almost every supermarket's doing it.
It happens many other places as well.

It's not that you don't know it's happening, there's just nothing you can do about it.

I know people who suffer from chronic fatigue, depression, have ended up in hospital and even killed themselves because of it.

Try proving something you have no evidence for!! It doesn't happen. You barely know who's done it.

How to do it:
Anyone who's watched a spy film would know this one.

It's super easy to buy some modern variation or even make your own. There are many variations. Chemist warehouse (in Australia) sells a particularly effective version. Some people call it Jungle Juice.

Pour a decent amount of the liquid on a rag you can breath through, hold it over a persons face until they pass out.

Watch a YouTube video of it, it works QUICK!!

Once they're asleep you can do anything you want. (scary isn't it!) As long as they're in pretty much the same position as what they were when you drugged them, and they can't find any evidence. They'll have no choice but to question them selves and just live with it.

What happens to them:
Un-conscious. Asleep.
You don't remember anything of what happened.

How to get over it:
I've heard people with tattoo's can't donate blood for some reason, also those who use recreational drugs, or those who are sexually promiscuous.

or ("let's not and say we did")

But...

Anyone for Revenge?

Depends how often it's happening to you? Always have your back against a wall.
When working on a laptop, sit with an open knife or a super sharp pen/pencil next to you.
(learn how to use/hold it, most people who pull a knife end up hurting themselves).

Put a barrel bolt on the door, so people can't sneak up on you when you're focusing.

It might be time to start carrying a flick knife, pepper-spray, a tayzer or handgun.
Become a Sikh or Jedi, they can legally carry knives everywhere (aka, a light sabre or kirpan).
Get a dog to guard you. (The drawback is they can also be drugged)
Get a smart watch that can call 000/911 if you pass out.

The aim isn't to use this stuff, just wave it around to scare people off. It's a deterrent. But be prepared to use it if you have to, junkies can smell fake.

Choose your company wisely!

Oh The Possibilities!

Conclusion:

Ok, So the conclusion of this book.

I hope you feel a little bit more empowered.

Hitting someone, or putting a knife in them will get you in big trouble.

And yelling abuse will make you look stupid.

You can get back at a stuck up bitch (men and women can both be bitches) without acting like an ape.

Plus, I hope you had a bit of a laugh at these ideas. I had fun brainstorming them.

Ultimately, if you can leave them, leave them, let them become a lonely old wench.

But if you're stuck there, have fun.

Karma's a bitch!

Notes:
(create your own)

- Hearing what someone says wrong, and getting them to repeat themselves.
(like they're name)
"Oh, hi John"
"No, its Tom!"
"That's what I said, John.."
just keep going with it. lol

- Using things when you know they'll be using them.
(like the Kitchen or the shower)

- Put extra soap in with their washing

- Ruin or hide their tools (blunten them, hide them, pens, paintbrushes etc.)

www.ingramcontent.com/pod-product-compliance
Lightning Source LLC
Chambersburg PA
CBHW011151290426
44109CB00025B/2576